About the Author

Steve Kay is a Business Management Centre in UK, wl̲ principles and practice of good ̲̲̲̲̲̲ship and management skills. His training tends to be highly interactive and humorous as he believes it helps students to enjoy and retain the learning experience.

For most of his career he was in the packaging and beverage industries. He spent 14 years with Coca-Cola, based in London, England, where he had European management responsibilities for packaging quality and development. His creative nature encouraged him to challenge the traditional role of technical groups and become more attuned to the marketing side of the business. He became Strategic Innovations Manager for Coca-Cola's European Development Centre.

Steve, who was married to Lin for 34 years and has a 31 year old daughter, Sarah, had to change his career when Lin became very ill with Cancer and MS. However, the move was a good one, as he loves training and empowering others to enable them to realise their true potential.

Note …This is a self-help book, but Steve is happy to facilitate "Charlie's Exercises" should you feel it would be beneficial.

The Proverbial Manager

Steve Kay

Illustrated by Clive Francis

Published 2006 by arima publishing

www.arimapublishing.com

ISBN 1 84549 156 4
ISBN 978 1 84549 156 7

© Steve Kay 2006

All rights reserved

This book is copyright. Subject to statutory exception and to provisions of relevant collective licensing agreements, no part of this publication may be reproduced, stored in a retrieval system, or transmitted in any form or by any means, without the prior written permission of the author.

Printed and bound in the United Kingdom

Typeset in Palatino Linotype 11/16

This book is sold subject to the conditions that it shall not, by way of trade or otherwise, be lent, re-sold, hired out, or otherwise circulated without the publisher's prior consent in any form of binding or cover other than that which it is published and without a similar condition including this condition being imposed on the subsequent purchaser.

arima publishing
ASK House, Northgate Avenue
Bury St Edmunds, Suffolk IP32 6BB
t: (+44) 01284 700321

www.arimapublishing.com

Dedication

I would like to dedicate this book to my lovely and remarkable wife, Lin, who throughout our marriage was a constant source of inspiration to me and also gave me the greatest gift of all, our daughter Sarah.

In fact, it was during her last critical illness (when she was sleeping or resting) that I wrote this book, and I am sure she would be so pleased that it has gone into print and that my thoughts and ideas can be shared with you. I really hope that you enjoy it.

My thanks also……

To Clive Francis, a truly great illustrator, who seemed to instinctively understand what I wanted and managed to capture the essence of Charlie in a comical yet realistic way.

The Proverbial Manager - Chapters

- 1. Why Proverbs? 9
- 2. Superstitions and Old Wives' Tales 23
- 3. Introducing Charlie… 29
- 4. Beyond Vision and Mission 35
- 5. Everyday Popular Proverbs 43
- 6. Using Proverbs in Your Business 61
- 7. More Proactive Proverbs Exercises 75
- 8. And Finally… 95

Features:

= Storytime

= Charlie's Exercises

Chapter 1
Why Proverbs?

This is a very odd idea isn't it? Running your business life by using "Proverbs," so let me try to help you to understand why. Firstly, what does the word mean?

Well, the Oxford Dictionary says:-

"Proverb – a short pithy saying in general use. One that is widely known."

The fact that it is widely known, is the reason why I believe it fits in just as well in our business life, as it does in our private life.

When I started researching this subject I found that there were literally hundreds of proverbs from all over the world. I must say, I was a bit surprised, to find that, it is not just the British who say things like:-

"Make hay while the sun shines".

Just imagine something similar being said in different countries and different cultures all over the world. You could say that it is a common language, that captures an idea in a few choice words, and allows those who hear it to instantly understand and interpret it.

In the rest of this book I want you to see how we can all capture and use both common and lesser known proverbs to help us, solve problems, develop our business skills, and to use them in an effective and often fun way for business communications, especially presentations.

One of my favourite proverbs is:-

"A watched kettle, never boils".

Of course this is not a true statement, as a kettle obviously does boil, but this is not the point. What it is indicating is that if you stand and watch something working, it seems to take forever, and does not appear to perform as well as you would like it to. To stop this negative feeling, you need to go away and leave it to get on with its function. When you do this, surprise, surprise, it takes no time at all to perform its function, and does it in a way that is perfectly satisfactory to you.

In a business sense, this can also relate to personal performance. It suggests that if you stand over your colleagues or those who report to you, when they are carrying out a task, you will never get the best performance out of them. In business, we call this **Micro-Managing** and it is something we all do, from time to time, but some managers do it all the time, because they are so scared of the consequences of delegation.

The, **"if you want a job done well, do it yourself,"** syndrome, becomes **"if you want them to do a job well, stand over them and make them do it your way,"** syndrome.

For the person being **Micro-Managed** it is intimidating, annoying and counter productive. The antidote to this behaviour, is to give your reports the knowledge and guidance to carry out the task, and let them get on and complete it, with as little interference as possible. They may not do it exactly the way that you would have, and they may make mistakes, but they will learn quicker and may actually find a better way of doing it than you…. heaven forbid!

Other areas I found particularly interesting were the proverbs that appeared to contradict each other like:-

"Fools rush in where angels dare to tread"

and

"He who hesitates is lost"

When we think about this a bit more, these two proverbs are not really contradictory they just relate to different types of situations.

For example, if you are a policeman and have been advised of an incident in an estate which has a reputation for a high level of violence, you should not **"Rush in"** without understanding more about the situation and arranging back-up to deal with the incident in a safe way.

On the other hand if you are at the sales and really have your eye on a bargain it is best not to **"Hesitate"** or someone else will jump in and snap it up and therefore **"All will be lost"**

You could say that use of proverbs is a matter of… **"Horses for courses"**

Another interesting aspect of proverbs is the way they have been amended to create a secondary proverb such as:-

"The early bird catches the worm"

but after modification…

"The early bird catches the worm, but the second mouse gets the cheese!"

Proverbs have a knack of helping us create vivid pictures in our minds of specific events. For example, after a rain shower, worms are encouraged to come to the surface of my lawn. The birds realise this and come down for some easy pickings. So, when I hear this proverb I can just imagine the bird, like the ones in my garden, tugging away on the worm with all its might. However, it appears to be such an effort sometimes, that it seems like the worm is trying to hang on for dear life under the earth as in the picture below:-

However, the poor old "first mouse" did not see the danger and got more than it bargained for, which left the "pickings" to the smarter "second" mouse who was not so impetuous.

Again as I have shown, the second mouse is feeling rather pleased that he let someone else "test the water" first.

In business both of these proverbs can be true, as some companies have prospered by being first into the market **("The early bird")**. However, this is only true if they have a strong business proposition or have developed a product or service that is very special or possibly patent protected.

Quite often, the first company does well for a while, but the second company on the block, who may be a bit more experienced, have more business muscle, or maybe, a better pedigree, launches a similar product. By being second they avoid the pitfalls (teething problems) that the first company has endured, and hence can become more successful.

Hence the **"second mouse"** gets the reward.

As I said, we often create mental pictures of what people say and so as you can see, I thought it would be interesting and fun to illustrate some of my favourite and more comical proverbs as you go through the book.

Well, let's face it, it is true that:-

"A picture paints a thousand words"

Humour, is something we all need, both in our private and in our business lives. It makes our lives and others', more enjoyable, and is a great way to relieve stress. Having worked as a trouble-shooter in multinational corporations it was sometimes the only way to survive!

On one occasion, when I was a trouble-shooter in the can business, I was called in to a major brewery to resolve a quality issue. The Quality Manager who, to avoid any embarrassment, we shall call "Dave", was a reasonable guy, but the quality issues were becoming too frequent for his liking and he wanted to lay down the law. Dave, however, spoke so fast and so long that his colleagues called him "machine gun". By the end of my meetings with him, my ears were often ringing and my head was swimming.

On this particular day, as I entered the factory, I was met by one of his supervisors.

"Hi Steve" he said, "in for your usual ear-bashing, then?"

"Looks like it" I said, raising my eyes to the sky

"Well, I'd like to share something with you before you see him. The guys and I have been talking about Dave and we reckon we have the ideal job for him. We think he would be a great Deep Sea Diver"

"Why's that?" I replied, feeling rather puzzled.

"Because he breathes through his bum!" he said, and burst out laughing.

I must say it was difficult to concentrate during the meeting with Dave, imagining him in his Deep Sea Diver's suit, but it did help me get through a stressful day.

I was therefore very pleased to discover some great humorous proverbs. You can see a list of the "best" in Appendix 2, but here are some that particularly tickled me:-

"A squirrel is a rat with good PR!"

Lets face it, squirrels may look cute, but don't forget that they are still rodents and are pests in their own right.

In business, I am sure you have met one or two "squirrels". These are people who seem to have great charisma, are smartly turned out, and instantly become your best friend and confidant. In fact, they are very good at lulling you into a false sense of security. However…

Before you know it, they pinch your nuts, and show you what total rats they are!

I bet you **now** recognise someone in your organisation that fits this description!

Another interesting one is…

"A camel is a horse designed by a committee"

We have all been there haven't we? You start off with a great idea for a new product but by the time everyone has put in their two pennuth, you end up with something you just don't recognise. Unless one function or person has overall authority, a hybrid of marketing, production, and finance, plus the CEO's particular preferences, is created.

My personal favourite that needs no explanation is:-

"Beer is proof that God loves us and wants to make us happy"

I'm not sure if this is a true proverb, but it works for me!!

And then there is also the rather whimsical….

"A spy with flatulence always blows his cover!"

Yes, I know, I've lowered the tone already, sorry!!

There are also some more obscure proverbs like…

WHY PROVERBS?

"A bird can sing with a broken wing but you can't pluck feathers off a frog"

Er, yeah, answers in a brown envelope and send to my publisher please!!

So now it is time to get serious, well almost, I feel strongly that humour helps learning, as students on my business training courses would confirm, so I will subject you to the odd bit of fun as we go through the book.

I expect you to enjoy and see value in the process, but if it's not for you, at least you can have a laugh or two as you work your way through it!!

Chapter 2
Superstitions and Old Wives' Tales

In the 1950's and 60s I grew up in the English, Hertfordshire village of Knebworth. This was not Knebworth House, I might add, which in the sixties, became a centre for massive pop concerts in the UK, including the legendary Rolling Stones. In more recent times Robbie Williams had them flocking in for nights of great entertainment.

During my childhood and adolescence I remember my mum often quoting superstitious sayings. In fact, my life seemed to be run by them. I thought, at the time, that it had something to do with living in a village, but have since found out that every family has their own pet sayings.

We were never allowed to have an umbrella up in the house, and it would cause hysterics if a pair of new shoes were put on the table. As a young child I walked to school making sure not to walk on the cracks between the paving slabs and had to get off the ground when a train passed nearby. Apparently all of these things were to avoid having bad luck.

When I was courting my future wife, my mum got very excited when she "found" two teaspoons placed on a saucer as this apparently indicated a forthcoming wedding! Wishful thinking on her part I think, but she was right and I did get married, within a year, to my beautiful Lin.

Mum was also big in "Old Wives Tales" particularly in relation to keeping us healthy.

I don't know about you, but when I was a boy, I remember my mum insisting that my sister, brother and I had to have a tablespoonful of cod liver oil each week, because her mother had given it to her, and it was good for us (as well as making us feel decidedly sick!). I thought it was just an "Old Wives Tale" that had no facts to back it up, but it was easier to go along with it, than to upset her.

For a long time this practice seemed to have lost favour, but in the 1990s it become very popular again. In fact, in the 21st Century it's now "cool" to take Cod Liver Oil, as scientists believe it not only keeps us supple, young and active, but also supplies Omega 3 which helps children's' brains in the learning process. See my mum was right that fish was "brain food". At least fish oils can be taken in capsules now, which is a little more civilised than the old days!!

Some more of my mum's Old Wives Tales also had some validity such as: -

Feed a cold and starve a fever – It is sensible to feed a cold, as the body needs fuel and nutrition to fight the cold virus. On the other hand, a fever needs to be cooled and so more fluids are needed and feeding takes a back seat. Hence you "starve" it.

Eat carrots as it improves your eyesight – There is some scientific evidence to show that Vitamin A, as found in carrots, is needed for the health of the eye and for adaptation to dark conditions. Beta-carotene, found in carrots may also reduce the risk of cataracts. However the origins of this "tale" was that during World War Two, British intelligence didn't want the Germans to know that their pilots were using radar at night. Therefore they spread the rumour that the pilots were fed carrots to improve their vision!

On the other hand here are some of the ludicrous old wives tales I was subjected to in my youth:-

- **Eating greens will put hairs on your chest** – as a child I always wondered what happened to ladies who ate greens!

- **If you spill salt throw it over your left shoulder** – This is to blind the devil who is on your left shoulder and will take over your soul if you don't do it!
- **Breaking a mirror results in 7 years bad luck** – Whoops, there goes another one!

- **Find a penny, pick it up and all day long you'll have good luck** – Hmmm.

- **If you keep pulling faces it will stay that way!!** – well, that explains a lot!

- **Sitting on a dirty toilet seat can make you pregnant** – didn't affect me, but as I grew up I came to realise that men find it hard to get pregnant!

- **If a needle on a thread, held over a pregnant lady's belly, moves in circles, she will have a boy!**

As I said, every family has "pet" old wives tales. For example, my wife got very upset if we passed the salt seller directly from one person's hand to another's!? Apparently this is bad luck.

And if you thought tales only came from the dim and distant past, think again. I found these:-

- Using lottery numbers according to your pet's or your family's birth dates will increase your chance of winning

- You should wear gloves when handling floppy discs in case you catch a virus!

So as you can see, superstitions and Old Wives Tales are not very often a reliable source of wisdom. It therefore makes it difficult to see how we can relate them into our business lives, other than to feed the human species' need to have superstitions.

Proverbs, on the other hand are almost always based on the experience of life, and are far more reliable, as a source of wisdom. They have also been a part of just about everyone's life in the UK and, from what I have discovered, the rest of the world, for as long as anyone can remember.

Proverbs are passed down from generation to generation in countries across the planet. I have listed some of the most common ones and some interesting and lesser-known ones, from different countries, in the Appendices. However, to list them all would require another book....now there's a thought!!

So unlike Superstitions and "Old Wives Tales", as most Proverbs actually make a lot of sense, we can easily use them in our business environment.

In the rest of this book I will show you how they can be used to cover a variety of areas. You will also be shown some exercises that you and your colleagues can use to help your businesses.
To keep it light-hearted I have created a character called Charlie who is the amalgamation of several people I have met and a bit of myself, but I am not going to reveal which bit!

You may recognise someone in your organisation who is a bit like him.

Chapter 3
Introducing Charlie...

As I have said, at this point, I would like to introduce you to a young man called Charlie. This guy was in a mess about a year ago, but had a "Road to Damascus" type of experience that changed him completely in both his private and business life.

Charlie had been to university and used his degree in business studies to help him join a successful multi-national company. Charlie, met Mary at university and married her soon after completing his degree. They live on the outskirts of London and plan to have children, "when the time is right", but not until after they have secured the big house and the BMW! For the moment they are concentrating on their careers.

Charlie was, at one time, considered to be a high flier, and had worked his way up to Brand Manager. However in recent years things had stagnated, and many of his colleagues were getting very disillusioned with his work style. They felt strongly, that he had been **"promoted to his level of incompetence!"**

As a Brand Manager he was regularly involved in major promotional projects involving marketing and advertising agencies.

On this particular day, a year ago, he had a critical meeting with an agency at which his Director of Sales and Marketing would attend. Charlie needed to make the right impression, as this Director did not **"suffer fools gladly"**.

Charlie had a heavy night, the night before, and had slept badly. Just as he was falling off to sleep, the alarm went off and immediately seared through his head and started shredding his brain. After a few choice words Charlie jumped out of bed and started running around like the **proverbial,** "headless chicken".

First he grabbed his clothes, then rushed into the bathroom, showered, dressed, then threw a coffee down his throat, or that was the plan. In his haste he missed his mouth and spilled coffee down his shirt, causing him to scream and rush back to the bedroom to change his shirt and tie. He then grabbed his briefcase and flew down the stairs and out of the door.

Slamming the door behind him, he felt the relief of being on his way. That is, until he reached the car and discovered, to his horror, that he did not have his car keys, or any keys, for that matter.

He let out another scream, ran back to his front door, and rang the doorbell continuously until his poor wife, who was keen to have an extra hour in bed, was forced to come down the stairs and let him in. He charged past her, spurted into the bedroom, shook the keys out of the trousers he had worn the day before (sounds familiar??), and charged back down the stairs and out the door. On his way out he muttered that he was now running late and Mary said something less complementary, which he didn't hear, but she'd make sure he did when he got home!!

Ready to start again he opened and entered his car, reversing it out of the drive at high speed and knocking over part of next door's wall, before squealing off down the road where he drove straight into a traffic jam!

He now realised that he would definitely be late for the meeting, but at least everything else was okay. Well, when I say okay, he had managed to wear one brown and one black sock and, oh yes, the tie he grabbed earlier was the one that he spilled his soup down the night before…oh my God!!

The upshot of the morning's disaster was that Charlie:-

- Was still late for the important meeting

- Had upset his boss

- Looked a disgrace and was the subject of ridicule from his peers ("a proper Charlie" they kept saying)

- Damaged his Company car

- Upset his neighbour

- Had to face his wife when he got home and grovel to her to get back into her good books

What a great day!!

When Charlie reflected on his day the proverb ...

"MORE HASTE, LESS SPEED"

came to mind.

What a pity he didn't think of it before!

Charlie didn't realise it at the time but this was to be a **defining moment** in his life. The knowledge gained, and actions taken, following this incident, moved him, within a year, from a bumbling embarrassment of a man to a competent and likeable member of the human race.

The effect on his work was dramatic and in this book we will pass on some of his learnings, to help you in your specific work situations.

Like Charlie we all tend to think of a Proverb after things have happened. This is still useful especially if you can take it on board and learn from it, such as in Reflective Learning. This is a technique, which has become popular recently, especially in public organisations like hospitals, and I will explain more about it, later.

However, as you go through this book Charlie will show you how to use **"Proactive Proverbs"**, that will allow you to work more effectively and efficiently. You will also be given **Charlie's**

Exercises, to enable you to open up new thoughts for your personal, departmental, or company, critical business issues.

Chapter 4
Beyond Vision and Mission

In the 1980's and 90's there was an unstoppable movement in large Corporate Companies to create some understanding of where they aspired to be and how they were going to get there. This was commonly shown in the formation and development of the company Vision and Mission statements.

Being in one of the largest Corporate Organisations, Coca-Cola, at this time, I was caught up in this approach that was sweeping through our company like a virus. I was a Packaging Development Manager in the European Development Centre in the mid Nineties and it was felt, by our senior management that we needed a Vision and Mission to help us develop ourselves especially as there had been changes in the structure and overall management of the group. We needed to demonstrate to ourselves, and those outside, that the group had a clear purpose and way of achieving it. We were due to have a group meeting and so this would be incorporated into the agenda.

The Group HQ was in Brussels and our team members were based in Germany, Spain, Belgium and UK. It was decided therefore that the meeting should, of course, be held in the Champagne region of France!

As you can imagine we in the UK were absolutely devastated by the location as we had all set our hearts on Grimsby!!

However, we had to bite our lips and girth our loins in preparation for our journey across the channel so that we could seek enlightenment.

Once there, we quickly got into the swing of things and after the odd glass of champagne and a few more beers we felt enthusiastic about the tasks ahead. We spent about 3 days discussing the structure of our group's various factions and our role within the vast Coca-Cola organisation. We also had to understand how our individual teams related to each other and with the outside world.

A good day of our time was dedicated to what I call **"contemplating your navel"** where we developed the whole group's Vision and Mission as well as our specific team's Vision and Mission. We were enthused, eager and motivated to get it right and to give direction and purpose to our group. We were very satisfied with the results. The champagne and relaxed environment also helped to give us this feeling of euphoria and well-being and so we relished the thought of carrying this "new world" back with us.

Our office had been in Kensington in London when I first joined them, and was then moved to Hammersmith in the west of the city in the early nineties. Although I lived in Luton, only 35 miles away from the office, it still took me the usual 2 hours to fight my way through traffic on my first day back. On my way in I remember being very positive about our new beginnings and I had lots of good thoughts on how I would incorporate it into my work pattern both personally and with my team of Packaging Engineers.

On my arrival I turned on my computer and saw that I had over 100 e-mails waiting for me. I also checked my voice mails and discovered another 18 messages (I had cleared them the day before). I let out a sigh, and my chin dropped and I felt the need for not just one, but two high strength coffees, before attacking the challenges set before me.

That day I can honestly say, seemed a million miles away from Champagne, and the expression, **"Back to reality"** was soon in my mind and my lips. I was not alone in this sudden change in demeanour as two of my colleagues expressed the same opinion.

You see, it is not that we wanted to change back to the old world, it was that life had been different whilst we'd been cocooned away in France, whilst real life had continued in the usual way in London, Europe and Atlanta and was waiting to mug us as we came through the doors!!

It is very important that an organisation has a Vision of what it wants to be, and that all the employees understand and buy into it.

The idea of having a Mission, was also very understandable as you have to have a route map to achieve the Vision. The problem is that Visions are often pretty obvious things like:-

"Our Vision is to be the best, most creative and most successful IT company in the world"

Fine, and how do we achieve this? – cue the Mission statement:-

"We will employ the most capable people in the industry, to create innovative new products, and marketing strategies. We will add value to the whole system, through our skills and our focus on customer service."

This is a mission statement, I created in just 5 minutes, but it includes most of the "right buttons" we need to press:-

- Great people

- Creative products

- New Marketing approaches

- Adding value

- Customer focus

It probably needs some work, but one thing it has that most Mission statements have, is that it asks more questions than it answers, like:-

- How do we get these great people?

- How do we become more creative?

- What will our marketing strategies be?

- How exactly will we add value?

- What do we do to become customer focussed?

Every working day we are beset by challenges and demands on our time, minds and decision making abilities, and quite frankly, the Mission statement is not the thing that immediately springs to mind. It has to compete with far more pressing everyday business issues like:-

- How will I get this report finished on time?

- Why is my boss acting like a 4 year old?

- How can we overcome this quality problem?

- How can I motivate Joe to work harder or smarter?

- How can I stop e-mails killing my time?

- How can I cover my rear end on this one?

- Why do I have to play office politics?

Oh, and I almost forgot…

"Will I actually get to see my family tonight or even this week!!"

We need to deal with these types of issues in a way that is not alien to us, but may actually open up new ideas and approaches to everyday or longer term goals.

So what have Proverbs got to do with this?

Lets face it, if you talk to your colleagues and ask what the company Mission statement is, you will be lucky if 30% answer with any accuracy. Now, if you ask the same people to quote you two Proverbs, I can predict that at least 90% will be able to do so. We are familiar with Proverbs and so using them in a business environment can also be perfectly understandable.

The people "at the coalface" are the ones who have to deal with such issues as:-

- Irate customers

- Under achieving suppliers

- Fire-fighting problems

- Unrealistic deadlines

- Interpersonal issues within and outside of the organisation.

They need to quickly assess situations and come up with solutions that not only fix the present but also build the foundations for the future.

On analysis of these issues you can use Proverbs to set the strategy and initiate actions, that will help bring about solutions to these problems.

It can be used to encapsulate what is going wrong and be a springboard to a creative approach to overcome the issues and strengthen the company.

Proactive use of Proverbs can also help to deal with such strategic issues as:-

- Leadership skills

- Objective and goal setting

- Optimising work processes

- Problem solving

Chapter 5
Everyday Popular Proverbs

As we have stated already we all know and use proverbs to explain particular events. Here are some of the ones that quickly come to my mind:-

- A stitch in time saves nine

- Too many cooks spoil the broth

- A bird in the hand is worth two in the bush

Let's look at how these may enable you to help yourself, your department or your company.

"A stitch in time saves nine"

Literal meaning

As we can see in the above cartoon, Charlie has got himself in a rather embarrassing situation again. Mary had been telling him that his trousers looked a bit frayed and either needed repairing or replacing, but he knew best. By literally not putting **"a stitch**

in time" he was now showing all and sundry, his rather poor taste in boxer shorts!

What do we mean by this proverb in a wider sense:-

- Procrastination is the enemy of good decision making and timely progress

- Dealing quickly with a small issue or problem can prevent it becoming a major issue in the future

So let's see how we can use this to help us in business:-

What's in it for you?

- It can prompt you to think about how you use and organise your time. Look at areas where there is or has been procrastination. This could prompt you to employ simple Time Management techniques to enable you to get things done and make good decisions at the same time. The whole concept of what is urgent and what is important can be addressed.

- It can prompt you to organise and manage Projects in a more effective way by dealing with problems or changes as they occur and not leaving them to grow into major issues

What's in it for your team/ department?

- Interpersonal issues are often an area where a **"Stitch"** can prevent things getting out of hand, especially behavioural issues. By not dealing with a minor discipline or guidance issue early on, it can build up with this person until it becomes a major problem, which would be much more difficult to deal with. This can create a bad situation with the person involved, and if not handled well, can also have a bad effect on the rest of the team. You could say that, **"One bad apple spoils the barrel"**

- Your people are looking to you to give leadership but if you procrastinate, especially over something that is perceived by your team, as a straight forward decision, you will lose credibility and possibly respect by the team or particular individuals

What's in it for your Company / Organisation?

- In many companies especially within manufacturing units it is very important to reduce quality issues. How can you approach this? Well, thinking about **"A Stitch in Time"** in relation to this, one of the approaches is the incorporation of Statistical Process Control as part of the manufacturing control system. This process helps manufacturers to identify trends in their operations so that intervention can take place **before** the quality issue occurs. "Prevention is better (and less expensive) than cure."

- There are strategic times in all organisations where **"A stitch in time"** is vital to the short or longer-term health of a company. Two of the major areas are:-

Reorganisation - By looking at all functions of an organisation and analysing their efficiency and effectiveness it is possible for companies to identify issues that are detrimental to the organisation. There may be bottlenecks, duplications, or outmoded operations. There may also be people issues or technology gaps. By looking at this closely and taking appropriate action to counter them, the senior management of the organisation can improve the effective use of all functions.

Rationalisation – We all know about this word, and to be honest, it tends to make us think of negative or even cynical thoughts and remarks. As an employee it is often seen as an excuse to shed people, due possibly to earlier management incompetence, but it is very often the lack of **"A stitch in time"** that is the downfall of many, previously successful, companies. Senior Managers need to consider where the company is heading or why the results are perhaps not as good as they should be.

Do not be fooled by the previous statement, as even companies that are still considered highly successful, have to be rationalised. The reasons can be numerous and can include reduced profits, reduced market share or worrying share value. It could also be that there needs to be a move to the core business, if diversity has damaged the profitability or image of the company. Once the cause has been identified, actions will need to be put into place as quickly as possible (i.e. **"a stitch in time"**) to reduce damage through procrastination.

During a merger or takeover there is often a need for rationalisation to take place as quickly as possible. Any delay can cause confusion and uncertainty with employees, shareholders, customers and suppliers. Therefore, although it may seem harsh on those affected it is for the long term good of the rest of the employees that this takes place and is completed as quickly as possible.

In my time in multinational corporate organisations I have experienced both sides of this situation. Being made redundant can be a painful experience, but if approached in the right way can actually be beneficial to the individual in the short or long run. Sometimes those made redundant had been fed up with their existing jobs and were contemplating moving anyway. If you are really lucky, as I was, you can pocket the redundancy and walk straight into another job. It could also allow them to look at the situation and decide if this is really a career path for them or might they use their skills more effectively in other areas. They may even have been contemplating early retirement, anyway.

Being one, who is retained in the company during a redundancy period, can also be a double-edged sword. On the one hand you are pleased not to lose your job and there may be good prospects for you in the revised organisation. On the other hand you have to live with an uncertain work environment and your workload will most likely be increased significantly.

No-one would suggest it is a pleasant experience, but most times, in most companies, Rationalisation is justified.

"Too many cooks spoil the broth"

"Hubble bubble toil and trouble"

Let's consider an actual, kitchen scenario:-

It is a real problem in any kitchen, if several chefs each believe that they know how to produce the best broth and approach the task together. One adds a bit of salt and another adds some herbs, another turns the temperature up another turns it down, then one wants to thicken it up and another wants to thin it down. It is a recipe for disaster!!! (please excuse the pun)

To prevent this, what happens, in well organised kitchens, is that either the head chef takes charge and demands that it be done his way or he/she delegates the broth to one of the assistant chefs who has accountability for the final result.

What does it mean to us in business?

- We need to control who and how many people have direct input to a particular process or project and designate one person who has overall responsibility and accountability.

- We need to be organised in such a way that we ensure the task is completed in the most effective and efficient way.

What's in it for you?

- **It can help to hone your leadership skills such as delegation** – looking at the skills you have available to you it is necessary that you delegate tasks. However, delegation, without good guidance can often end in chaos and confusion. Marry the task and the person responsible, wisely.

- **Helps to clarify your roles and responsibilities** – by using the "Too many cooks" approach you will learn to plan out a task and realise that, at the end of the day you have overall responsibility

What's in it for your team/department?

- **Helps create a structure within your team** – as with all teams there may be a natural hierarchy either in an ongoing way or dependant upon the specific situation. The allocation of accountability is therefore of critical importance.

- **Helps allocate team's roles and responsibilities** -some of your reports may be particularly good at creative thinking, whilst others are more practical and can convert ideas into reality. It is important to use these strengths for the benefit of the team. This may also be an opportunity to develop those areas that are weak within your team.

- **Planning and managing resources is identified** – as in the kitchen the planning and managing of both people and equipment / technology is very important. A successful project is not about throwing lots of people at it. The identification and designation of specific tasks for different individuals is vital. However all could be lost if the work is not well co-ordinated so that it is effectively implemented.

What's in it for the company/organisation?

- **Streamlining of the Company functions and management structure** – companies start off with a set structure but over the course of several years this can change dramatically. If this change is beneficial and in response to market changes all well and good. However, sometimes the changes are historical, or even hysterical, and can be more related to particular individuals or functions "empire building". It is important, therefore, to revisit this area and see if it is actually beneficial or detrimental to the company as a whole. If detrimental, streamlining or more radical changes need to take place.

- **Problem solving** – Very often, especially if there is a very expensive and damaging quality problem that has taken place, companies tend to throw lots of people at it. The idea is that if you use the "scatter gun" approach, you will find the reason for the fault, quicker. In reality, this tends to complicate the process and delay getting to the "root cause". People are often concerned about diverting the blame, jumping to conclusions without properly verifying the facts, or allowing emotions to take over. I found that as the quality claim got higher so did the emotions. A £100 quality problem was easily settled, a £1000 was a bit trickier, but when we got to £1,000,000 how people changed!! One or two well trained troubleshooters, who are logical thinkers, can quickly identify what is happening, when and where it is happening, and how much is involved, rather than going off at all sorts of tangents, that lead to dead-ends. I was lucky enough to be trained in logical problem solving (Kepner Tregoe) and was very concerned that, during a claim, we concentrated on the facts, and not peoples' pet opinions or assumptions. **"Too many cooks"** can certainly be detrimental to this process especially if the "cooks" are inexperienced or insecure!

- **Organisation of the company under the "too many cooks" philosophy -** by looking at the overall operation of the company, senior management can identify where too many managers ("cooks") are spoiling the business objectives ("broth") and therefore action needs to be taken to rectify this.

The "**Too many cooks**" proverb can also be particularly helpful when managing large and complex projects.

"A Bird in the hand is worth two in the bush"

As you might tell from this cartoon, Charlie's interest in "Birds" was not just with the feathered variety!!

What does it mean?

- If you have something of value, it is best to hold onto it, rather than chasing after something that may "fly away" as soon you get near to it. You may also lose what you had hold of, or at least, damage that relationship that has taken you such a long time to develop.

What's in it for you?

- **Don't spend all your time chasing after vague opportunities, but look at the strengths you already have and use them well** – for example, you may feel that you would like to improve your computer skills and this is a perfectly legitimate thing to do. However, what you have to be careful of is that, for example, if you are a good two-way communicator, the more you start contacting your colleagues, by e mail, the less you are able use your traditionally strong verbal skills. This may be perceived by your colleagues, as you becoming more remote and damage the rapport and trust you had with them. As we all know **"Perception is reality"** so don't damage the very thing they respect you for whilst trying to develop new skills.

What's in it for your team/department

- **Look at what skills you have in the group and nurture them for the benefit of the whole team** – successful teams are very often forged from very different individuals working together with complementary skills. Although we need to stretch our reports we must make sure that their value to the team is encouraged through activities that require their particular skill strengths.

What's in it for the company?

- Don't spend all the company promotional effort in chasing new customers as you may lose the ones you already have. Good customer service to existing customers is vital to the long term health of the company. I remember when I was in the can business saying to one of my colleagues.

"Sales may secure the business at the start of the year, but Customer Service maintains it the rest of the year"

- It costs a lot more to gain new customers than to keep existing ones. The cost of regaining lost customers is also very high.

In 2002/3 financial organisations such as banks and building societies were so concerned in getting new customers, by offering them special rates and discounts on mortgages and other services, that they forgot who were the most important ones in maintaining the health of their business (i.e. their existing customers). Customers were, historically, reluctant to move from one bank to the next (I have been with mine for over 30 years) and this loyalty was being taken for granted by these financial institutions.

However, the existing customers, seeing what was happening felt badly treated, compared to new customers and so some were tempted to switch to other banks with better deals. This created fluidity in the system and an uncertainty that had not previously existed.

In 2004/5 some Banks and Building societies, realising that they had created a real problem for themselves started advertising the same special rates and discounts for existing customers, as for new customers.

Now, at last, they were looking after **"A Bird in the Hand"**, as well as the **"Two in the Bush"**!!

Chapter 6
Using Proverbs in your Business

As I stated at the start we all know Proverbs and we tend to quote them after an event has happened. This is fine and can be a good way of reminding ourselves of the way we should act in future.

Many public organisations are introducing Reflective Learning techniques, which help employees to identify what they did in a specific situation and write it down in a log. They then ask themselves to Reflect on this incident and note down how they would do things differently in future. This is a very fancy way of saying "lets learn from experience", but the formal way in which it is carried out makes it more likely that they will retain the learning, and therefore reduce the likelihood of mistakes being repeated.

However, the best way is to use proverbs is proactively. We will call them, rather surprisingly, Proactive Proverbs!!

How do we use Proactive Proverbs?

As a company or organisation we can use them as an ongoing commitment to the way in which we want to operate. You could call them the **Philosophy Proverbs** of the Company/Organisation and it works like this:-

At the back of this book you will find lists of proverbs from which you and your colleagues can choose those that you feel epitomise your company. By completing the following exercise you can then come up with 3-5 that you can use as your **Philosophy Proverbs.**

- Choose up to 6 –12 people in your organisation from different work functions

- Split into 3 groups in different rooms or out of earshot from each other

- Each group needs to look at the same list of Proverbs (chosen from the Appendix in this book) and choose 3

Proverbs that they feel fit best with their view of what the company should stand for.

- Alternatively the groups can be given different lists. The lesser known or comical proverbs could be used with the common proverbs to stimulate original thought

- The 3 groups come together and share their Proverb choices and the reasons why they have chosen them

- A total of 3-9 Proverbs will have been chosen.

- At this stage the group discuss the merits of each Proverb and reduce (if more than 5) the list down to 3-5.

- These proverbs now need to be combined in such a way that all employees can associate with the messages they convey as related to their everyday work situations

For example, if we choose the 3 Proverbs:

- A stitch in time saves nine
- Too many cooks spoil the broth
- A bird in the hand is worth two in the bush

We need everyone to understand the importance of these proverbs and so we need some explanation such as the following:-

The 3 Philosophy Proverbs of the ***** Company

- **A stitch in time saves nine** –It is important that if we see a problem starting in any aspect of our business that we deal with it early rather than hoping it will go away. The sooner we deal with the issue the less time and resources it will require. If this involves customer issues or problems, our quick action will also reduce the risk of aggravating, and possibly, alienating them.

- **Too many cooks spoil the broth** – Make sure that you have the right structure for responsibility and accountability so that our business can run effectively and efficiently. This is particularly important with customers where an understanding of the key contact(s) is clear to both parties. This is critical to reduce both duplication and / or confusion.

- **A bird in the hand is worth two in the bush** – Let us identify our core business and the strengths we bring to this area. Any move into other, speculative areas, must not be at the detriment of our core business.

The company, having agreed its overall **"Philosophy Proverbs"** needs to communicate this to all functions within the organisation. The purpose of this is to get everyone **"singing from the same hymnbook"**. Although this can be done using e-mail, it can be detrimental to the process as this is primarily a one-way communication tool. To add validity to the process, as well as discussion and ownership, it is useful that this outcome is shared with staff, face-to-face.

The most successful way of reinforcing the "Philosophy" is to have the above statements typed up and displayed at everyone's workstation as an "Aide Memoir".

For example, we are all guilty of putting things off and can come up with plenty of reasons why. So when the next bit of correspondence hits our desk or computer screen, we need to consider if a **"Stitch in Time"** would save us a lot of grief in the future. If the answer is "yes" then action needs to be taken right away. If not, then deal with what really does need urgent attention, and plan to deal with less crucial correspondence at a later stage.

Another way of reinforcing the Company Philosophy, is to share this with your customers and suppliers.

Why suppliers ?...well, if they understand more about the way you want to operate, then, if they are wise, they will take that on board when dealing with you in the future.

So, how can I as a manager or a professional use Proactive Proverbs?

Let us once again consider our friend **Charlie.** He was in a pretty bad state after the "meeting debacle" described earlier. As a Brand Manager, he realised that he had not done his own "Brand Image" much good in the eyes of his boss, his peers and the agencies he needed to deal with, as well as the most important "senior manager" i.e. his wife.

When he got home from the office after the disastrous meeting it was late and he was feeling very sorry for himself. He was hoping Mary would be sympathetic to his plight ...was she hell! He just got through the door when Mary hit him with a tirade of abuse along the following lines:-.

"What's the matter with you Charlie, you charge around like a madman, all the time, and seem to have no idea what you are doing. You knock things over, including, by the way, next doors' wall, for the third time, this year! You are like a "Bull in a China Shop" in this house, and from what I can gather from your colleagues, it doesn't get any better at work. You have become a cartoon character in your own lifetime. I can't relax around you and to be honest I am getting so stressed out, that we just can't go on like this. This is your last chance Charlie, either you sort yourself out or get out of my life!!"

Wow, not exactly mincing her words was she? Initially Charlie was angry with Mary and thought that she was being very unfair. However, after a suitable amount of self-pity time, he realised it was the wake-up call that he needed. He also realised that his life was way out of control. He didn't want to lose Mary, or his job, which he had to admit, was also looking decidedly dodgy, so what could he do?

He thought about what had happened yesterday and realised that this was not a one off. His life and work had been dogged with these sorts of incidents. In fact, at his last company his colleagues nicknamed him "Frank Spencer", (a TV comedy character who constantly left a trail of chaos in his wake) and he could now understand why.

Charlie realised that he needed to look at the ways in which he operated and to do something about it.

The first thing he remembered was how the proverb **"More haste, less speed"** had jumped into his mind. Mary was right, he was always in such a tearing hurry that accidents happened, and also poor, impetuous decisions were made, without proper consideration. Instead of saving time it invariably cost him time, as well as his reputation and credibility. It was time to slow down a bit and give himself a chance to use the talent and skills he had.

So he decided that **"More haste, less speed"** was to be the first part of his new strategy,…but there were other areas that he needed to address before he could move on.

After some deep thought about the way he ran his life, he realised that he got on people's nerves both at work, and in his private life, by cutting across their conversations just so that he could get his point of view over. He didn't mean to do it, he just felt he had to say it, there and then, or the moment would be lost. He knew that some of his colleagues thought he was rude and loud and liked the sound of his own voice.

He had just shrugged this off, but now in his **"contemplating his navel mode"** he realised that this was a trait that needed to be addressed. He thought that the use of proverbs might help him remember his failings and inspire him to change.

He remembered a proverb, that John, at work, had quoted to him in a recent, heated argument, during a meeting:-

"A fool finds no pleasure in understanding, but delights in airing his own opinions"

How right he was. He had to stop talking and start listening a lot more. Charlie saw this as another part of his new strategy to improve his private and business life, in particular his relationships with others.

As things generally go in threes (superstitions again!!) he felt the need to follow this train of thought.

Not everyone at work disliked him, in fact, he was quite popular with some, especially for his outspoken views and comical ways. He thought about his three best mates:-

- **Fred** – now let me think, he's a bit of a jack the lad, and self-opinionated. He has a really funny, although sometimes sarcastic, sense of humour. It can get him into trouble and recently he had a verbal warning for constantly back-chatting the Marketing Director.

- **Fiona-** well now, she's been with the company for as long as Charlie could remember and although she was quite bright she never seemed to move up the organisation. She had got quite bitter and cynical about the company and was not averse to "bad mouthing" it, to anyone who wanted to listen…. but most didn't.

- **Harry** – he's always been known in the company as a bit of a "drunk". Always the life and soul of any company do and not afraid to make a fool of himself. There was a rumour that he was on a last warning and it was clear that responsibilities were being taken away from him. Harry was considered by most of Charlie's colleagues to have the **"Desk near the fire escape!"**. In other words he was on his way out.

So, these are my best friends, Charlie thought, and a right motley crew they are too. Not exactly go getters are they? As he thought more about this, another proverb popped into his head:-

"A man is known by the company he keeps"

Nice people though they seemed, they were not exactly the type of people who were going to improve his reputation. Mary had also commented, several times, on the company Charlie kept, and it was not surprising, that he had been out with Harry, the night before that ill-fated important meeting. In fact, Harry had persuaded Charlie to stay in the pub much longer than he had wanted to because "Don't worry Charlie, preparation is for idiots, and you are a genius!" **Charlie realised he was an idiot!!**

So what now?

This had been a sobering exercise for Charlie and so he now wanted to capture his thoughts in a way that would allow him to operate in a different way and satisfy Mary that he had taken her seriously. On one piece of paper he wrote the following:-

These are my 3 Everyday Work Proverbs

- **More Haste Less Speed** – take the time needed to think through what you want to do and how you are going to do it. Do not rush in, either physically or mentally, but stay in control of your actions.

- **"A fool finds no pleasure in understanding, but delights in airing his own opinions"** – When in conversation or in meetings spend more time listening and understanding other peoples' points of view or opinions before airing your own. Compliment others on ideas that you believe are good and let them know that you are amending your thinking accordingly.

- **"A man is known by the company he keeps"** – make sure that you associate with people who are likely to be an asset, rather than a detriment, to your credibility within the company. Be careful that you have genuine friends and not those who don't mind damaging your image.

Like Charlie you may work or act in a way that is not beneficial to you or the image you are wanting to convey, and remember…

"Perception is Reality".

If you cannot think of anything, immediately, think of recent situations you were in and how you acted at the time and whether it gave the image you wanted. You might want to remember a meeting, a conversation you were involved in or a problem that needed resolving. Alternatively there may have been an incident that occurred and you may feel you didn't handle it quite the way you would have liked to. You may even, like Charlie, remember a cutting or sarcastic remark from a colleague that everyone concurred with.

Write down your feelings as they come to you and some first thoughts on how you would like it to be in the future.

Now look at the list of Proverbs in the Appendix, firstly in the **Common Proverbs**, but do not ignore other sections as these may also provide a Proverb that can meet your needs. Look for proverbs that encapsulate your feelings and can inspire you to change this particular aspect of your attitude or work-life. Humorous proverbs can be useful as they are easy to remember and quote to others.

Choose the Proverbs, and, as shown above, put them in bold letters or in a distinctive colour ink (red, say). Then after each proverb put your own explanation of what it will mean to you in your everyday work situation.

When finished keep this with you as an "Aide Memoir", so that it can prompt you to act or react in a way that meets your new approach to your business interactions.

Chapter 7
More Proactive Proverbs Exercises

Appraisals or Performance Reviews

During performance reviews, in most companies, there is a section where our line manager looks at ways in which we can develop by increasing functional or interpersonal skills.

If you are a manager you will also be assessing your reports' performance and be introducing some sort of action plan to overcome some shortfalls in their performance.

In both of these situations it can be very useful to encapsulate the faults in the form of a proverb.

For example, Charlie's line manager believed that Charlie had shown, all year, that if he had just sat down and thought things through before acting, he would not have made so many costly mistakes. So, his line Manager could encapsulate this as:-

"Fools rush in where angels dare to tread".

Charlie did not want to be, or be seen as, a fool, and so this proverb prompted him to think a bit more before throwing himself into action

Within the Appraisal system, ideally the Appraiser and the Appraisee can agree a suitable proverb and supporting text.

Next time you are carrying out a performance review on one of your colleagues/reports use the above approach and see just how this can focus your colleague's mind on what can help him/her in moving forward using an easily remembered proverb.

Teamwork and Team Structure

Structuring and maintaining a highly effective and efficient team is one of the most difficult jobs in an organisation. As we all know, we may have a team, but the members are all individuals and so what works for one may not work for another.

Team structure is sometimes something that we have a strong input to (i.e. formation of a new team). More often, however, we inherit an established team and so have had no say in the way it was structured. It is important therefore that we, as managers, and more importantly, as leaders, identify each of the individual's skills and attitudes and understand how these fit in with the team needs.

We need to blend the team and use the specific skills the individuals have, to become as effective as possible. Interpersonal skills and traits play a big part in the success and enjoyment, or not, of any team. Sometimes team members can have totally opposed opinions on how to approach certain aspects of work and this can create friction or even animosity within the team.

Proverbs can be used in several ways to help the team dynamic.

Here is an exercise that can be of benefit to a Manager or team leader:-

Individual values

- Show your team members a list of common proverbs

- Ask each of your reports to write down two proverbs that they personally like and can associate with.

- Now ask them individually to explain why they like them and what they mean to them.

- Discuss the findings within the team and show how different people can see and approach issues differently
- Avoid being judgemental, but gather the information to help create an insight into others and allow team members to also see that…

"There is more than one way to skin a cat"

Team Values

- Ask all the team members to write down a proverb or two that they feel is appropriate and useful within a team environment

- Help them with a list of common proverbs, if necessary

- Ask them to explain why they chose their proverbs.

- Gather this information together to get a flavour of the overall team values

- Look for common themes
- Look at opposing opinions within the group and ask how these may be resolved or accommodated.

- Share your own, team values, in terms of proverbs, so that you see how it fits with the present team values

- Agree 2 or 3 proverbs that encapsulate the common goals of the team

- Close the open discussion and take away all the contributions from the team.

- Consider the areas of difference between individuals as part of understanding them and think about how this may have occurred and what you may wish to do in the future to change some of the attitudes when developing your team plan.

- Obviously do not discuss this in an open forum but develop an action plan and discuss possible changes with the individuals!

Appropriate use of skills

- From the Individual Values exercise, above, you may well unearth different people's learning and work styles through the proverbs chosen.

- Open a discussion with the team to identify what were the main functions of the group and the tasks carried out to achieve the team objectives.

- See how the proverbs chosen by individuals meet the functions and tasks

- Identify if there are skills gaps

- Identify unused or misplaced skills (i.e. if an individual is a strong verbal communicator why does he/she spend so much time writing reports and little time using the verbal strength for Presentations etc?). Typical of the syndrome...

"Square peg in a Round hole"

- Consider how you can better arrange the tasks for the team to fit in with the skill strengths you have

- Identify skills that all members need, to carry out there jobs successfully and where there are skill gaps, agree training etc, to rectify this.

Project Management

This is an area that is rife for the Proverb treatment as you can set the main targets and work ethics in terms of proverbs. To help you understand this better we need to go back to **Charlie.**

At the meeting that we referred to earlier in the book Charlie was advised by the Marketing Director that he was going to be responsible for a new Project to launch a new product, in a different pack type. He also informed Charlie that this was his last chance to show what he could do and if he messed it up serious action would be taken!

He was told to get on with it without delay as they needed to bring the product to market within six months. Charlie therefore arranged a meeting the following week. He invited:-

- Sales Manager – Fiona Davies

- Production Manager – Ted Dawson

- Technical Manager - Gavin Walters

- Logistics Manager – Andy Hamlin

On arrival Charlie thanked everyone for attending at short notice and then started explaining the reason for meeting. He advised them that this was a very high priority project and it was vital that they quickly identified the key factors to ensure that the launch was a success.

Not too many years ago a meeting with all of these different functions present, was very rare as most functions worked in "silos" so that they only interacted with other functions, as and when, they felt it was necessary. However, this caused a lot of friction between groups, as issues were not picked up until late on in a project, and could, and often did, derail them. Multi-skilled Project Groups were therefore introduced and proved to be much more successful.

There were still a lot of "turf wars" but at least issues were flagged up quicker. Marketing still generally thought that Technical and Production were just trying to "put a spanner in the works" at every opportunity. Technical and Production felt that sales and marketing lived in "cloud cuckoo land" and needed bringing back to earth. I am sure this is not unfamiliar to you! However, it was time to pull together and give the project the best chance of success.

The discussion started as follows:-

Ted: "Charlie, why the tearing hurry?

Charlie: "We were planning to launch later next year but have information that points to our main competitors launching a similar product. We want to get in before them and scupper their chances"

Gavin: "The product has been developed and is ready to be trialled, but we will need production time to check out how it performs at normal production speed and in the new package format"

Charlie: "Didn't know you were already on board, Gavin, would have been nice to been kept informed, but at least we are now, so never mind!"

Ted: "You know this is a busy time of year for us and trials can be very time consuming. I really need to minimise disruption, but if it has to be done, let's do it efficiently."

Fiona: "Six months is a short amount of time to get everything ready and meet the launch objective. We have a lot to prepare on our side. Do you have a list of the steps we need to take and any estimates on timing, Charlie?"

Charlie: "The purpose of this meeting is to understand the tasks and timescales from all aspects of the business. Let's look at what is necessary from a commercial and technical point of view and see if the timescale is feasible. I would ask however, than everyone have an open mind on this"

Andy: "If the packaging suppliers are ready we need to see how this fits in with the tight supply schedule they have already"

Charlie: "OK, it is obvious that this is going to get very complex and we need input from you all. I have been asked to act as overall co-ordinator, but it is clear that each of you needs to co-ordinate your own areas and keep me informed"

Fiona: "I think the most important thing is to consider the proposed launch date and then work backwards to see if all of the steps can be achieved in the timescale. If so, we keep the proposed date, but if not, we need Charlie to have the information necessary to advise the Sales and Marketing Director that a revised date may be necessary. We do not want a repeat of last year's promotion disaster, caused by unrealistic timescales. As a consequence of this bad preparation a good colleague of mine lost her job!"

"I don't know about you, but I would like to keep my job, whilst at the same time doing the absolute best I can for this project."

Charlie: "Okay I understand your concerns, but let's take a positive attitude on this, and start getting down to the tasks and issues we need to address, in order to make a success of this project"

As the meeting went on, many technical and marketing issues were flagged up and times allocated to addressing these tasks. The main points that came out were:-

- Timing for the launch was very tight but looked achievable, with a small amount of slack built in.

- They needed to formalise a Critical Path Analysis Chart and then a Gantt Chart of both the technical and marketing tasks so that all concerned could follow the plan and if necessary amend them. One person would be responsible for these chart amendments and distribution to all parties

- Co-ordination was going to be vital and points of contact need to be agreed between all functions

- Charlie was accountable for the overall Project, but individual functions would also be accountable for the identification and resolution of issues in their area.

- High-level communication skills would be required to enable everyone to know of any delays or issues that may occur. There would also be a need to meet regularly (at least once per month) and more so if any critical event took place.

- Flexibility and co-operation between functions was vital to meet the objectives

- There was a strong feeling that to achieve success they needed to help each other and not create a blame culture. Success of this launch could be very beneficial to them all so they needed to have team goals.

Charlie was very pleased with the progress that had been made and now wanted to create a philosophy around the project process. He advised them that he had recently used Proverbs as a way of focussing his mind on the way he wanted to work and it was really helping him. He shared his 3 personal work proverbs with the group and although they were sceptical to start with, they all agreed that Charlie had read himself well and there was some validity in this approach. They agreed that it was worth a try in using proverbs to convey the essence of this new project.

Charlie shared a list of Proverbs with the group, and also said that if the group thought there was one, more appropriate, then it was fine to include that as well. Considering the major factors that had come out in the earlier discussions the group came up with following 4 Proverbs:-

- **Time and Tide wait for no man** – as the schedule was very tight it was vital that everyone used their time well.

- **First things first** – the order in which tasks were completed would have a serious impact on how efficiently the project was run. Therefore clear adherence to the Gantt Chart Plan was required.

- **Many hands make light work** – each one of the group should be committed to share the load so that the project could progress in the right way whilst, at the same time, allowing everyone to get on with the rest of their work commitments, without major disruption

- **Any fool can criticise, condemn and complain, and most fools do** – everyone needs to put their efforts into dealing with issues as they arise and work with each other in a positive way to resolve them. A blame culture is not acceptable.

A copy of these Proverbs were given to each member of the group and Charlie asked if they would keep this at their desks to remind them of what had been agreed.

To say that the others were impressed, by Charlie, was the understatement of the year. They had all gone to the meeting expecting his usual noisy, arrogant, and chaotic approach, but came out amazed at the control and professionalism he had displayed.

Next time you are asked to manage a new project or an ongoing activity see if it you can introduce the idea of capturing the way you want to run things in terms of Proverbs.

Like Charlie, you may find, to start with, that people are sceptical and think it is just another gimmick, but it is fun to do, and can bring out some interesting thoughts on the dynamic of the group and the activity being covered.

Doing this can also create something that is needed in all successful ventures and that is ownership by each and every member. If something is just dropped on you and you are expected to just go along with it, this can be de-motivating. If, however, you have participated in the process and agreed on the way things will be managed you are more likely to be enthusiastic about the challenges ahead.

Proverbs for Presentations

You know what it's like…
"You wait ages for a bus and then two come at once"

Well this is what Charlie thought when he had requests for two presentations, one on **"Budgetary Control"**, and one on **"Competition in the Market place"**.

Charlie knew that with presentations you need to quickly connect with your audience and get your point across well. In the past he had used quotations from well-known business people or celebrities. This time he thought that he would continue his Proverb theme and use one on the first slide of each presentation to give the right impact.

He thought about Budgets and then looked at the list of proverbs to see what would be appropriate. Firstly he thought of the most obvious:-

- "Look after the pennies and the pounds will look after themselves"

Not bad but not very original…..how about?

- "A fool and his money are soon parted"

Better, but I don't want to call my colleagues fools…I know…

- **"A banker is a fellow who lends you an umbrella when the sun shines, but wants it back the minute it starts to rain"**

Yes, that's nearly it and I could relate it to our accounts department who are notoriously stingy. Wait a minute the problem is not about saying that we need to control the budget, it's about doing it. So what we need is…

- "Fine words butter no parsnips"

I can then follow this up by saying "We all say that we need to control our budgets but saying it is not doing it and it's time we did"

Great now lets consider my next presentation on

"Competition in the Marketplace"

How about…

- "A bird in the hand is worth two in the bush"

Okay, but today's talk is about new business so not really appropriate. How about appealing to their egos…

- "Adversity doesn't build character, it reveals it"

Yes that is good and could fire them up for the challenges ahead. The only thing is I really want them to start thinking smarter about getting business. I know…

- **"Two dogs fight over a bone and the third runs off with it"**

I could support this by saying, "Sometimes we spend so much time doing the obvious thing and fighting competition over the same rewards, that we miss a new competitor coming on the outside waiting for the opportunity to outsmart us"

Yes that will get them "thinking out of the box" and open up new opportunities.

Charlie was pretty pleased with his opening proverbs, how about you…

We all have to do presentations at some time or another. Maybe you have one coming up soon and an opening proverb could help you. Have a look at the lists in the Appendices and see if you can find the right one.

Remember if you are talking to an audience, unless it is a very serious subject, a more light-hearted proverb may get them smiling and on your side.

If you do not have a presentation imminent then find some good proverbs for the following subjects

- Customer Service
- Leadership
- Teamwork

Chapter 8
And finally...

By now you may have had your fill of proverbs, or like me you have become a Proverb-holic. As I stated at the start of this book, proverbs are something we have all been brought up on, so introducing them to your business life should not be too strange. In fact, they are so well known that very often we only quote part of them and know that everyone will understand what we mean and finish the saying for us:-

- Don't count your chickens...

- A stitch in time...

- There are none so blind...

- Fools rush in...

Now that we have opened your mind to this use of language I can assure you that you will hear people using proverbs, at home, at work, on the TV (in fact, I heard five used last night). They are just about everywhere, that conversations are taking place.

AND FINALLY...

It's like when you are thinking of buying a new car that you believe is not driven by many people. As soon as you have bought it they seem to be everywhere on our streets. It's not that things have changed, it's just that you notice them, now that you have an interest, and involvement, in this type of car.

You may even be so hooked that you will have a **"Proverb of the week / month!"**

Thank you for reading this book and good luck with the exercises. Choose the ones that suit you best, and I would recommend you do your own personal one, like Charlie, first. I would also encourage you to practice them regularly, with your colleagues, so that it becomes a natural process in your organisation.

So goodbye from Charlie and from me, and all the best for your personal and business life, but whatever you do, please remember...

"If life deals you lemons, make lemonade!"

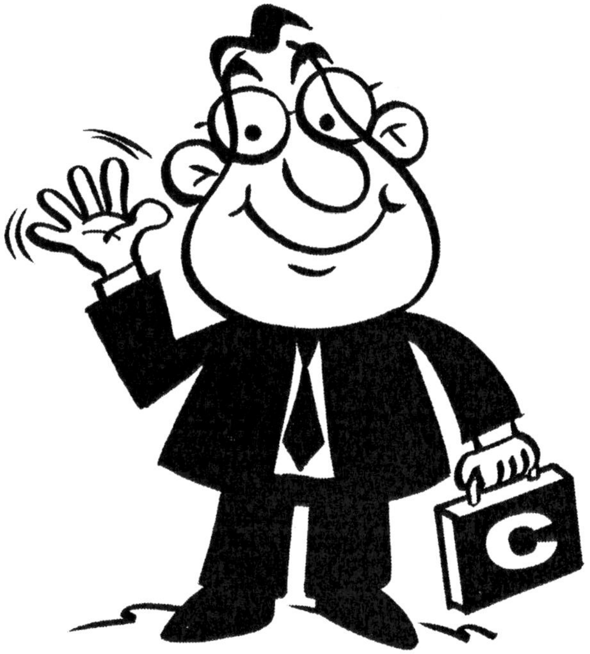
C

Appendix 1 - Common Proverbs

- A bad workman blames his tools
- A bird in the hand is worth two in the bush
- A chain is no stronger than its weakest link
- A fool and his money are soon parted
- A fool finds no pleasure in understanding, but delights in airing his own opinions
- A journey of a thousand miles starts with a single step
- A man is judged by his deeds not by his words
- A man is known by the company he keeps
- A new brush sweeps clean, but the old brush knows all the corners
- A picture paints a thousand words
- A stitch in time saves nine
- A watched kettle never boils
- Action speaks louder than words
- Adversity doesn't build character, it reveals it
- All good things come to those who wait, but only what's left by those who hustle
- Any fool can criticise, condemn and complain and most fools do
- Attack is best form of defence
- Better an open enemy, than a false friend
- Don't teach your mother how to suck eggs
- Don't count your chickens until they are hatched
- Every picture tells a story
- Familiarity breeds contempt

- First things first
- First impressions last
- Fools rush in where angels dare to tread
- Forewarned is forearmed
- He who dares wins
- He who makes no mistakes, makes nothing
- He who hesitates is lost
- It takes one bad apple to spoil the barrel
- Kill two birds with one stone
- Make hay while the sun shines
- Many a true word is spoken in jest
- Many hands make light work
- More haste less speed
- Necessity is the mother of invention
- No man is an island
- Nothing succeeds like success
- One volunteer is worth 10 pressed men
- Procrastination is the thief of time
- Smooth seas do not make skilful sailors
- Softly softly, catchee monkey
- Still waters run deep
- Strike while the iron is hot
- Take care of the pennies and the pounds will look after themselves
- The early bird gets the worm, but the second mouse gets the cheese
- The proof of the pudding is in the eating

- There are none so blind as those who will not see
- There is more than one way to skin a cat
- There is no such thing as a free lunch
- Time and Tide wait for no man
- Too many chiefs and not enough Indians
- Too many cooks spoil the broth

Appendix 2 - National & Comical Proverbs

- A banker is a fellow who lends you his umbrella when the sun shines but wants it back the minute it rains
- A bird can sing with a broken wing but you can't pluck feathers off a frog
- A camel is a horse that is designed by a committee
- A person who can smile when things go wrong, has found someone to blame it on
- A single conversation with a wise man is worth a month's study of books (Chinese)
- A spy with flatulence will always blows his cover
- A squirrel is just a rat with good PR
- As useless as a chocolate teapot
- Bad is never good, until worse happens (Danish)
- Beer is proof that god loves us and wants us to be happy
- Better to remain silent and appear a fool than to open your mouth and remove all doubt
- Do not use a hatchet to remove a fly from a friends face
- Don't speak unless you improve on silence
- Every path has a puddle
- Everybody's friend is true to none (Norway)
- Fine words butter no parsnips
- He who asks, is a fool for five minutes, he who doesn't ask remains a fool forever (Chinese)
- He who knows little often repeats it. (Brazil)
- He who attempts too much seldom succeeds (Norway)
- If life deals you lemons, make lemonade

- It's not the same to talk of bulls as to be in the bullring (Spanish)
- Learn to say no, its more useful than Latin
- Milk the cow but do not pull off the udder (Greece)
- People who think the world revolves around them, have no sense of direction
- Sometimes the majority means all the fools are on one side
- The cobra will bite you whether you call it cobra or Mr Cobra
- The earth does not shake when the flea coughs (Austria)
- The most beautiful women are made for lovers who have no imagination
- The old believe everything, the middle aged suspect everything, and the young know everything
- The world is full of willing people – some willing to work and others willing to let them
- Those who play the game do not see it as clearly as those who watch
- To bend bamboo start when it is a shoot (Malaysia)
- Two dogs fight for a bone and the third runs off with it
- When you shoot an arrow of truth, dip its point in honey (Arab)
- When two elephants fight it is the grass that suffers (African)

Printed in the United Kingdom
by Lightning Source UK Ltd.
115919UKS00001B/106